This Coloring Book Belongs To:

_____

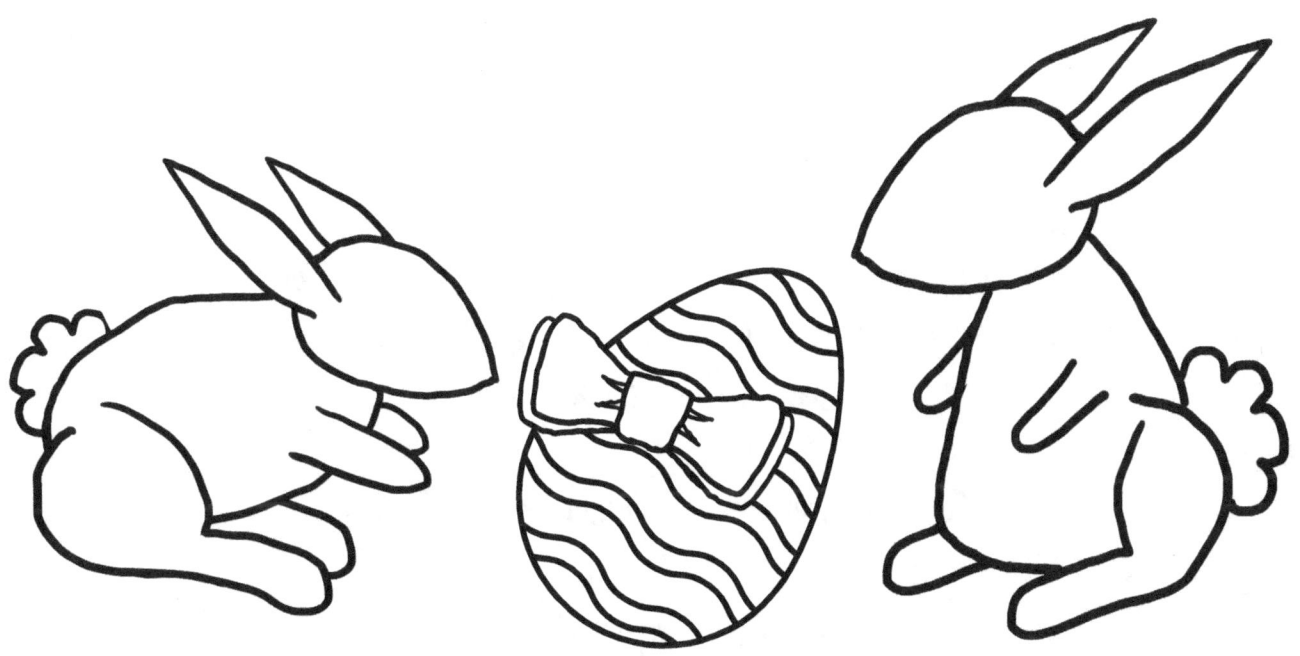

design.paulyeatman.net.au

Cover, illustrations and design by Paul Yeatman.

Ebook ISBN: 9798719615677.

HAPPY EASTER

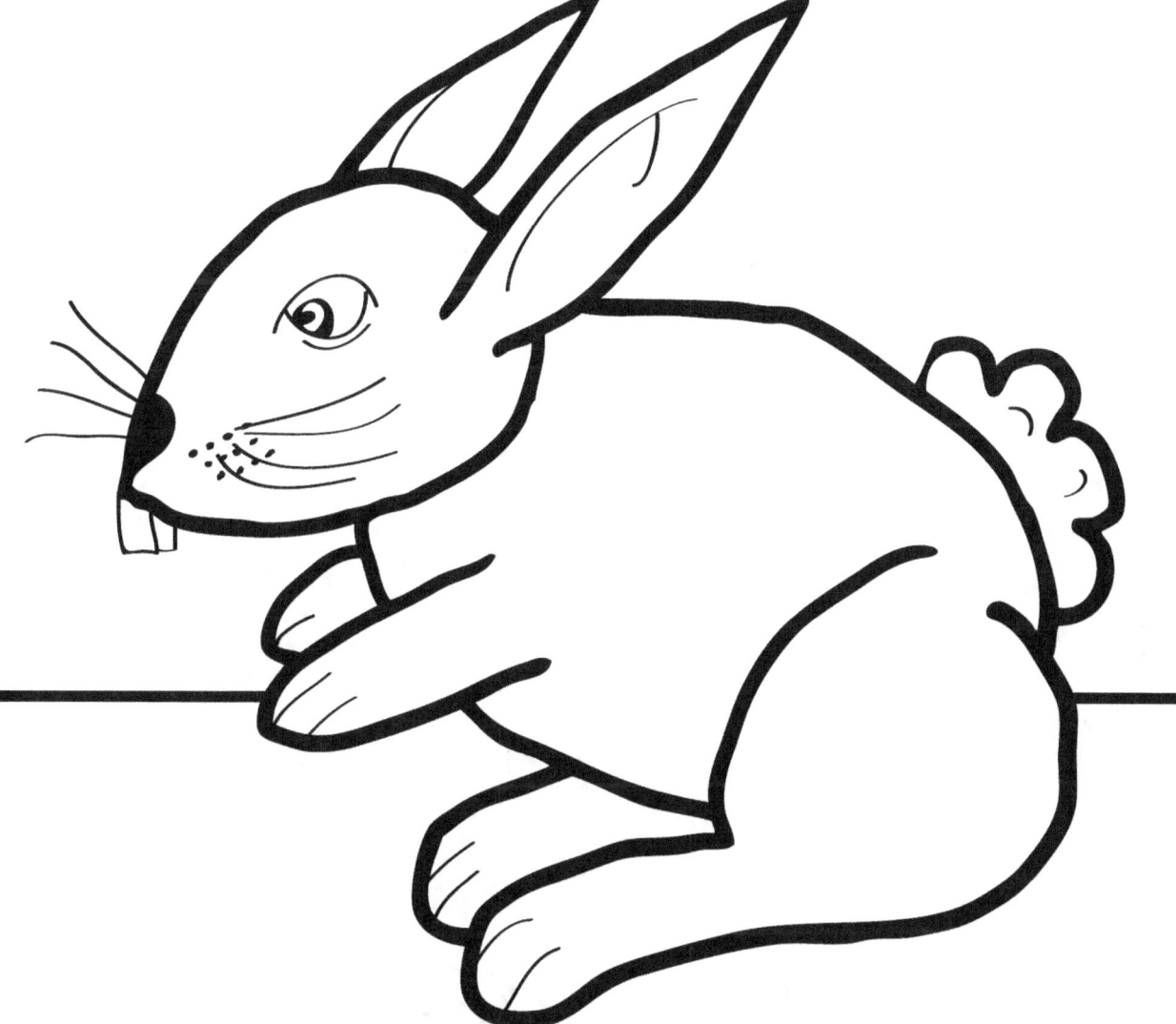

"Happy Easter: Bunny"

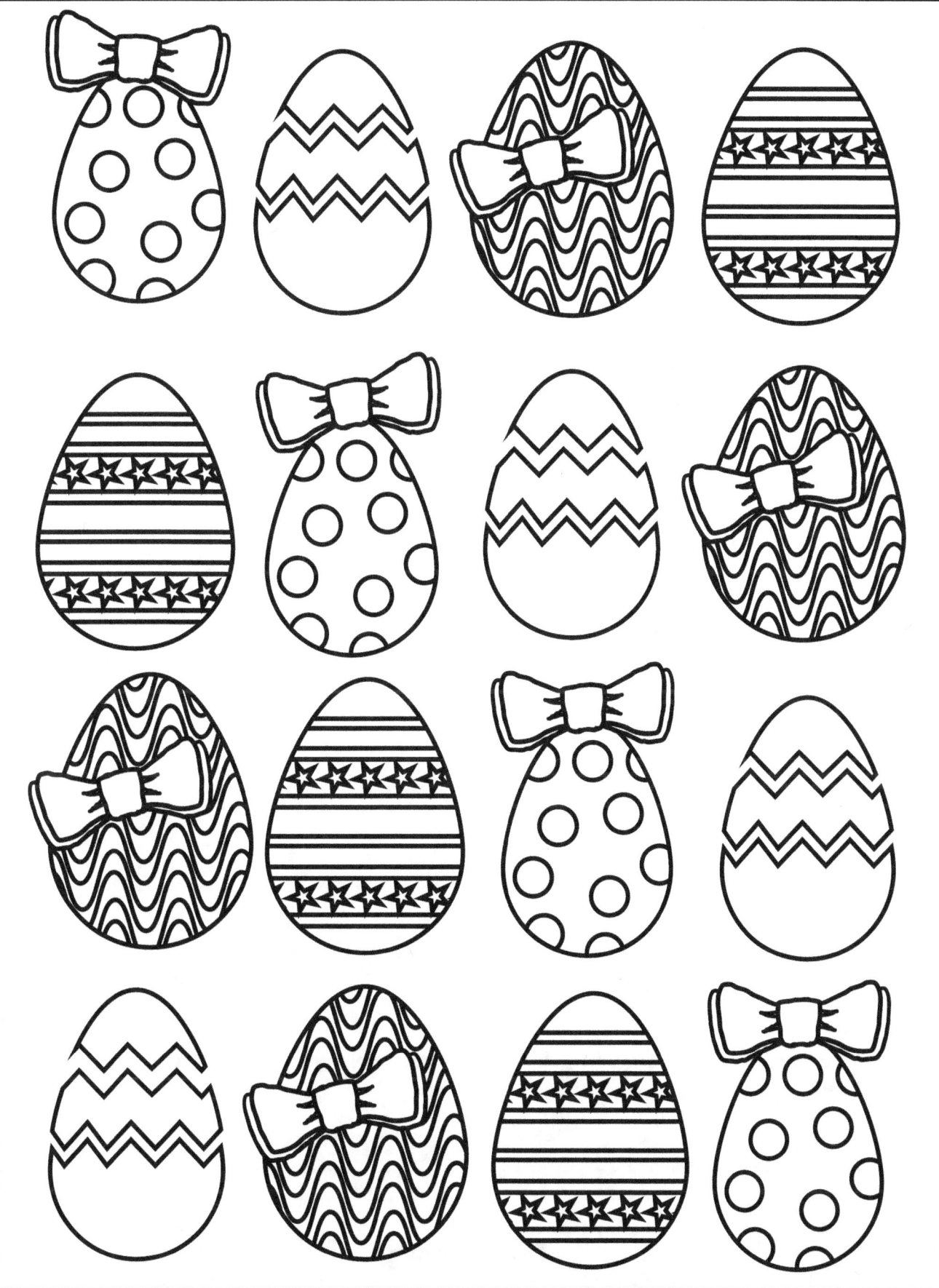

"Egg Spread"

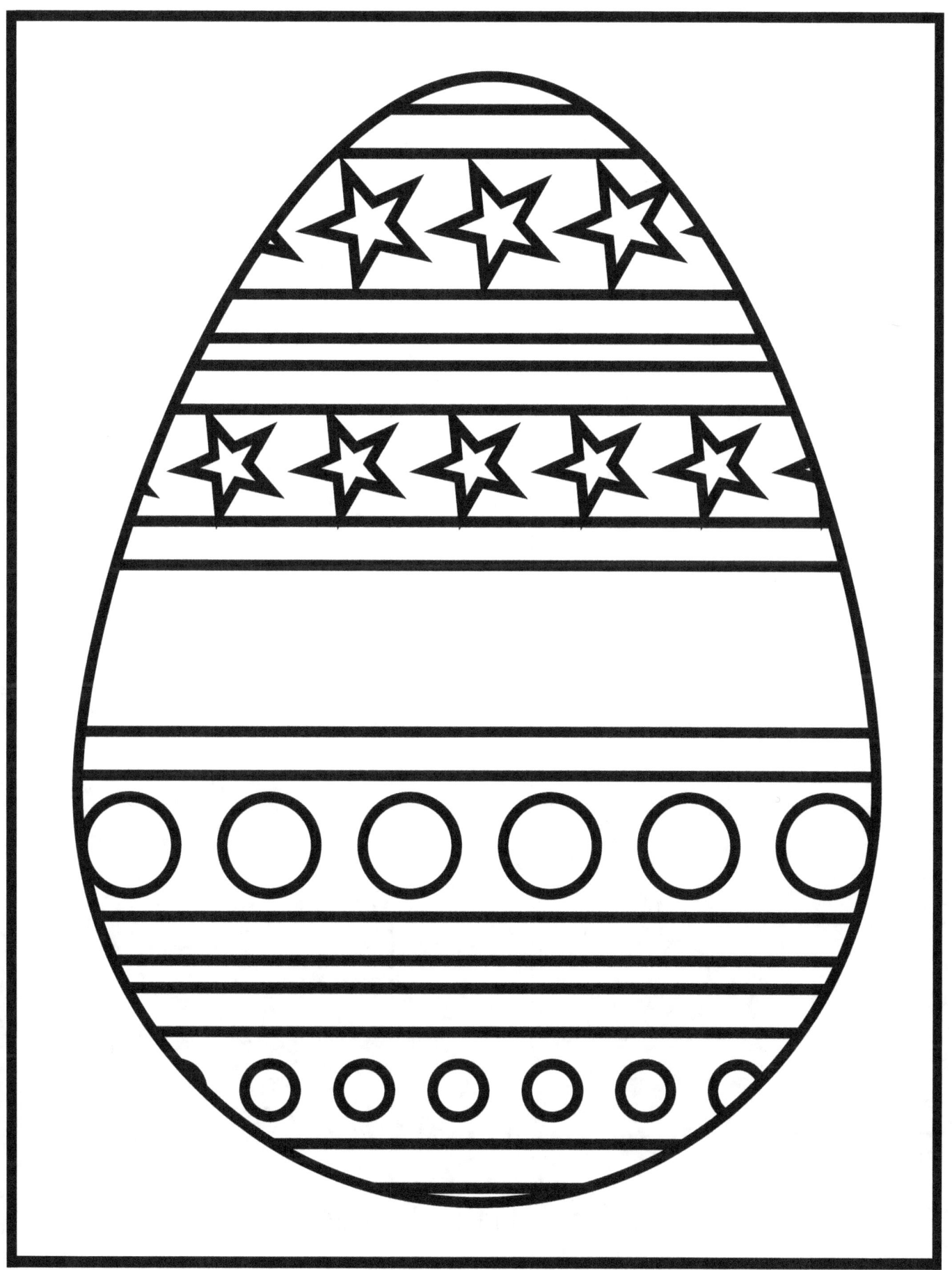

"Stars And Circles Egg"

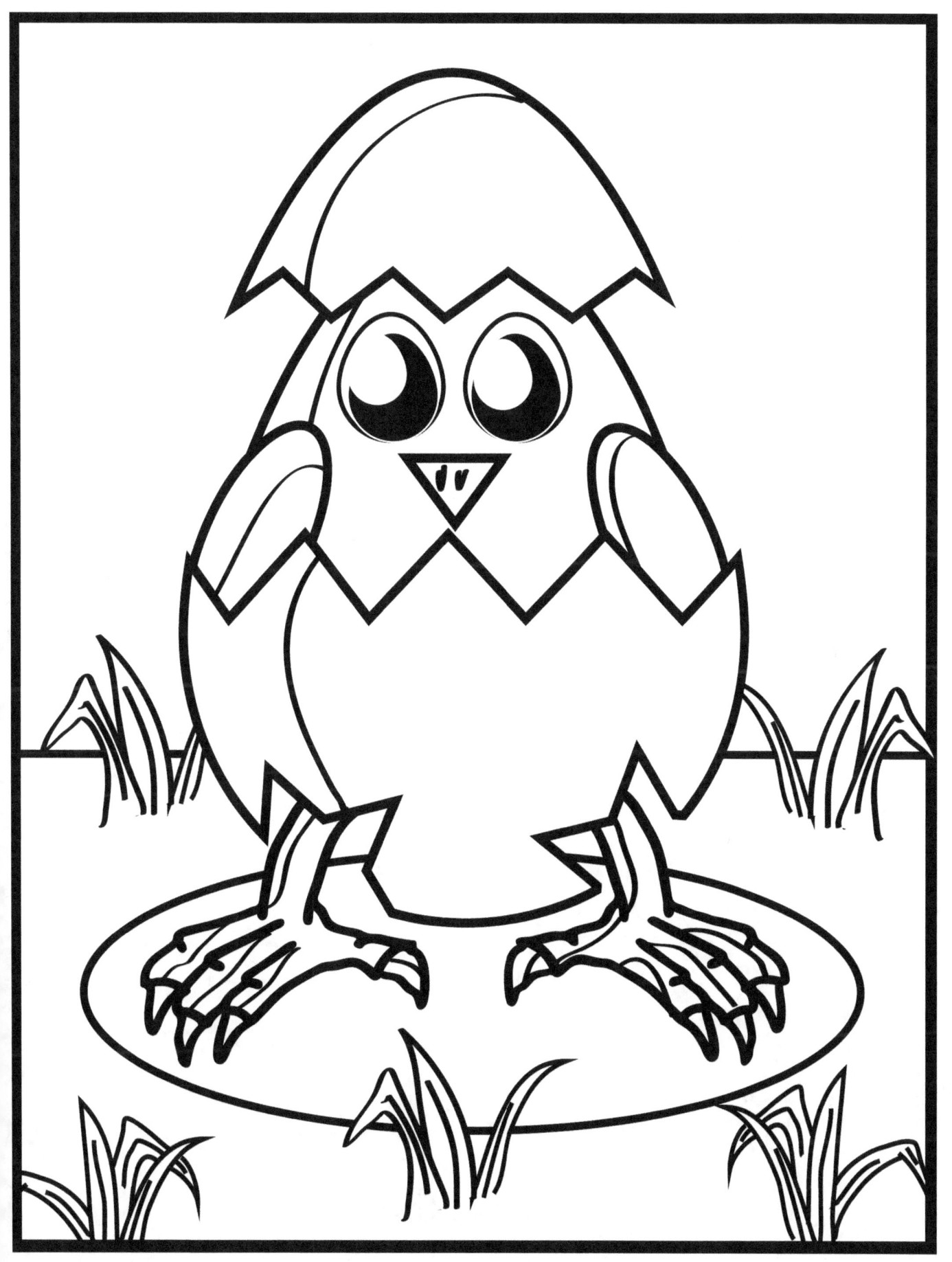

"Hatched Chick"

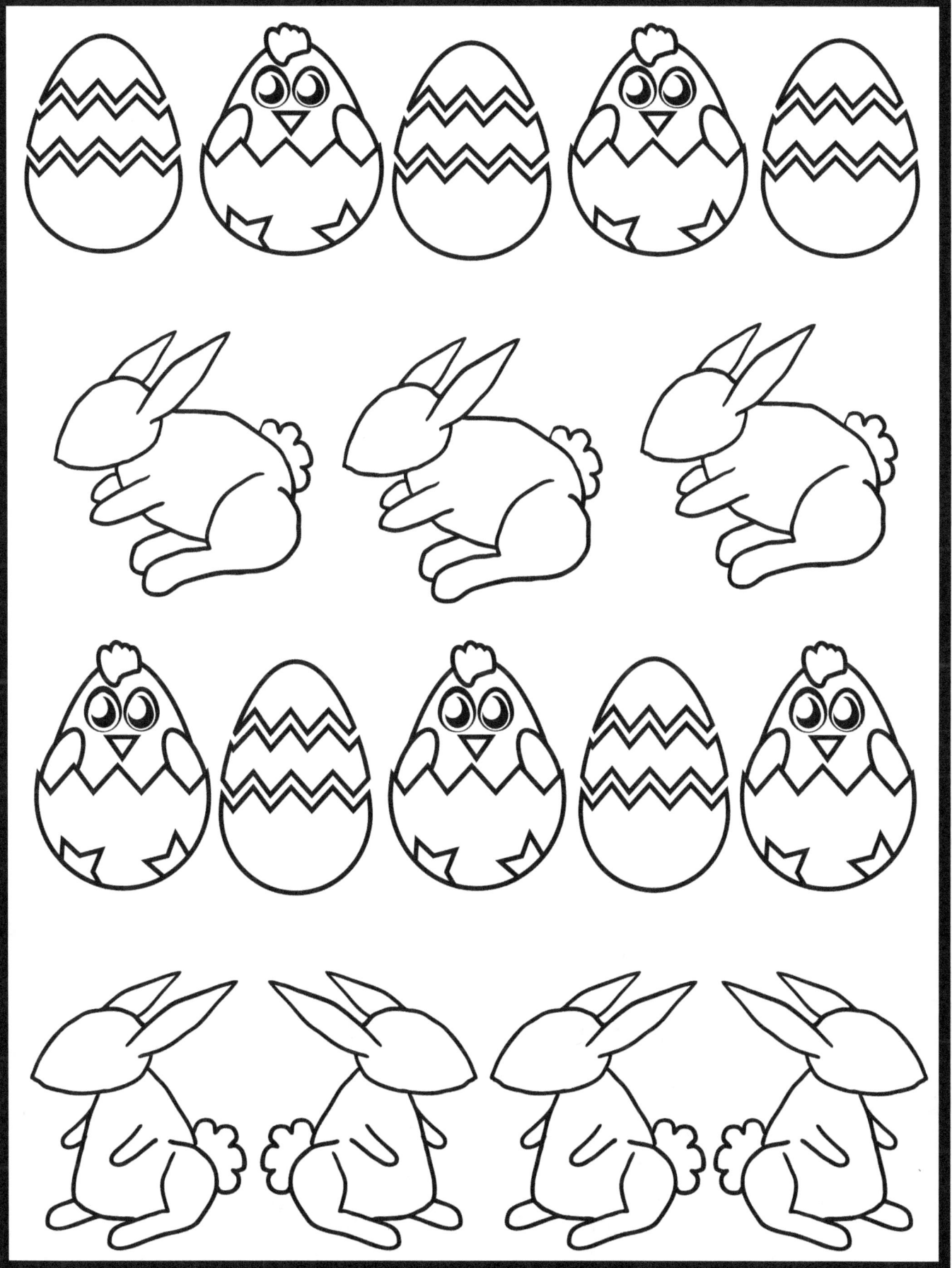

"Bunnies And Chicks Pattern"

HAPPY EASTER

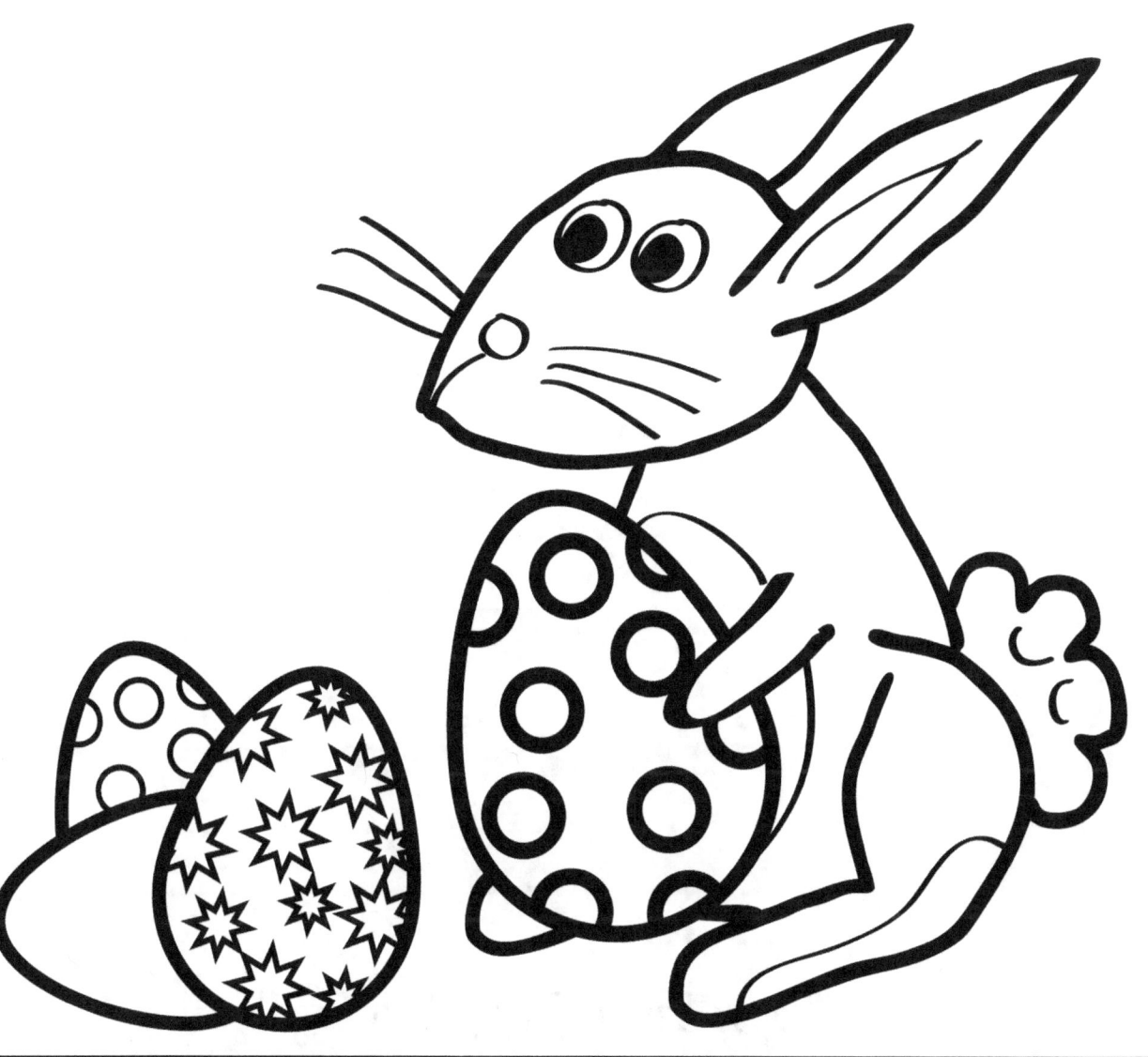

"Happy Easter: Bunny With Eggs"

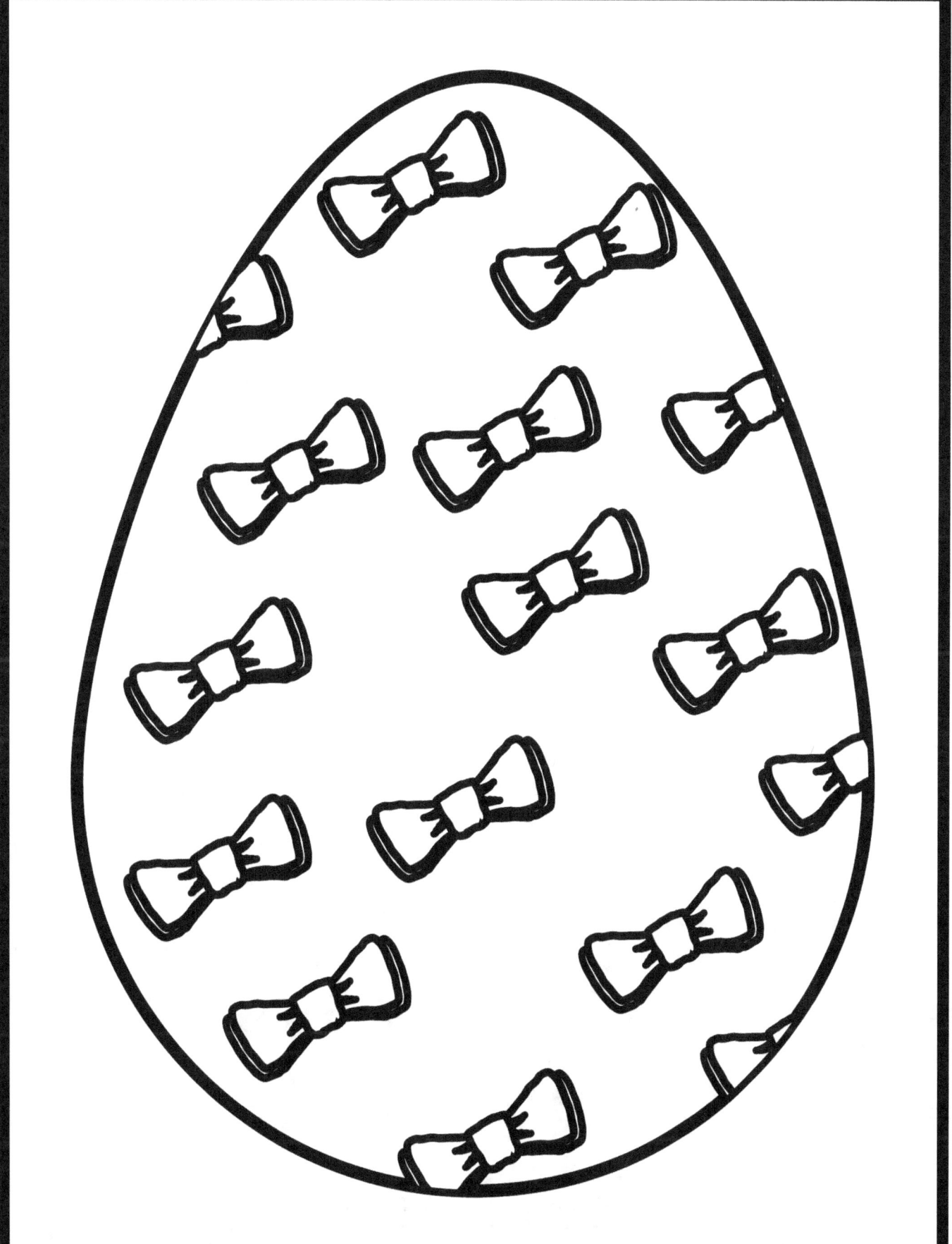

"Egg With Bow Pattern"

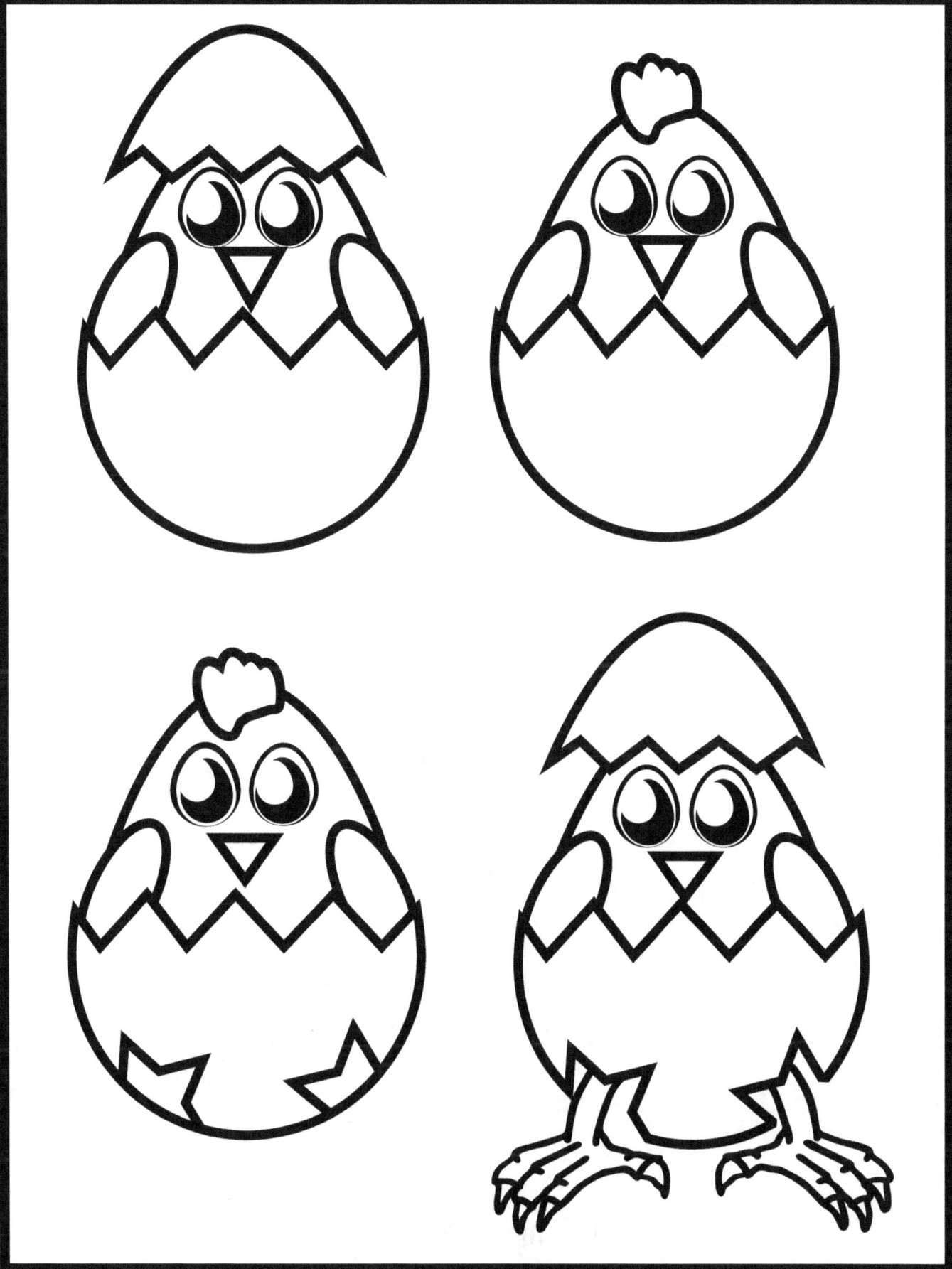

"Hatching Chick Sequence"

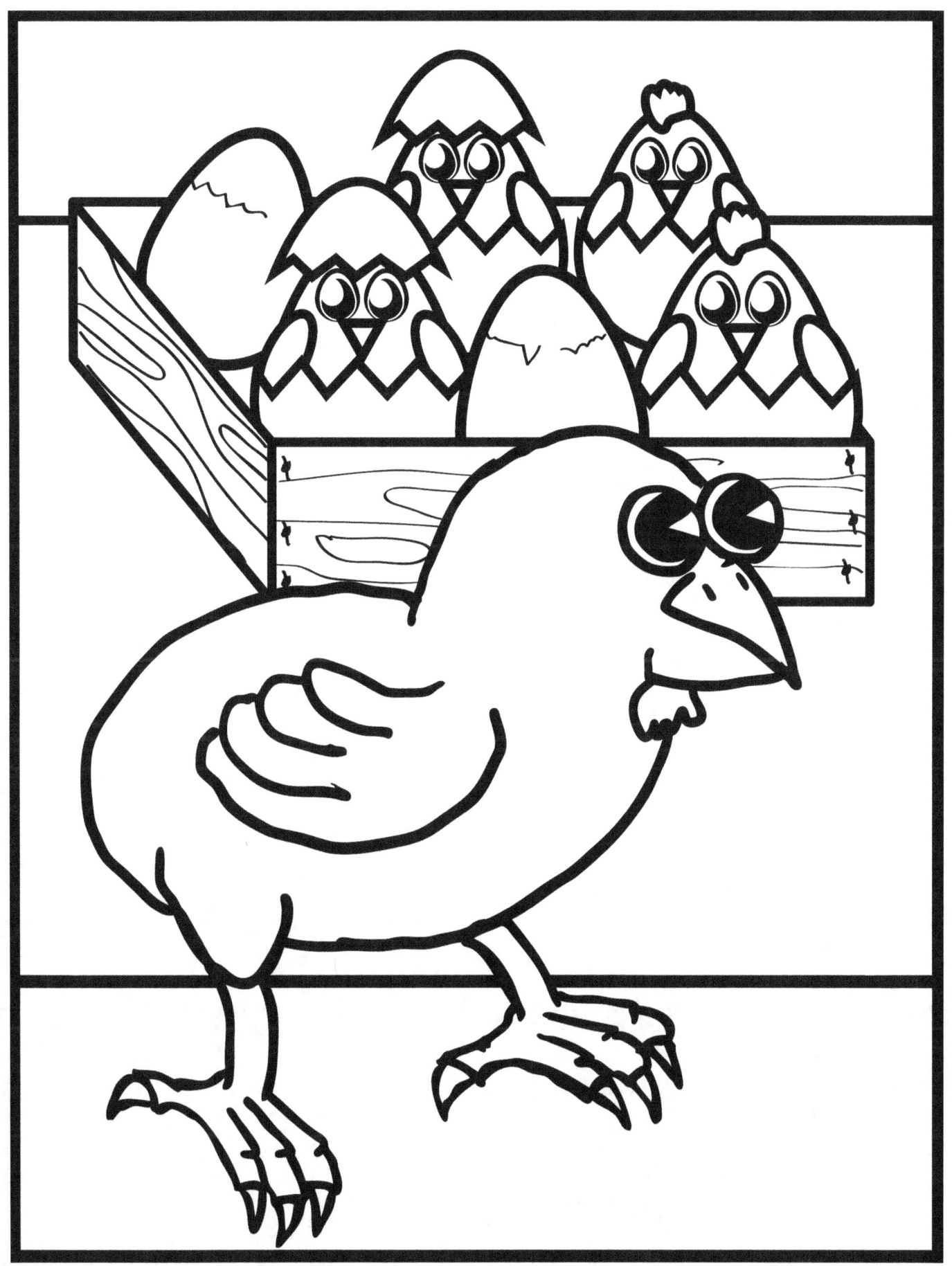

"Chick With Hatching Box Chicks"

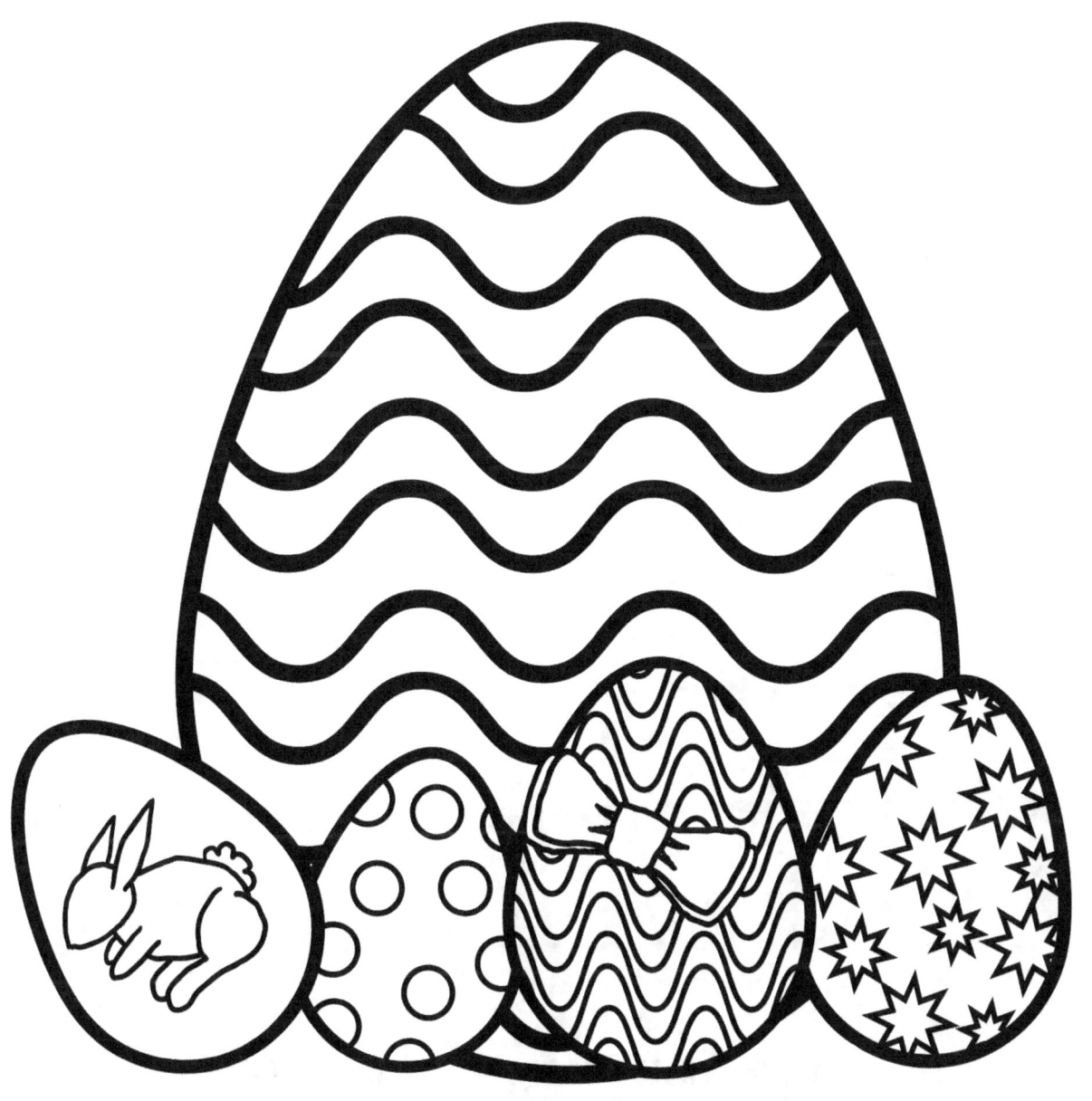

"Happy Easter: Large And Small Eggs"

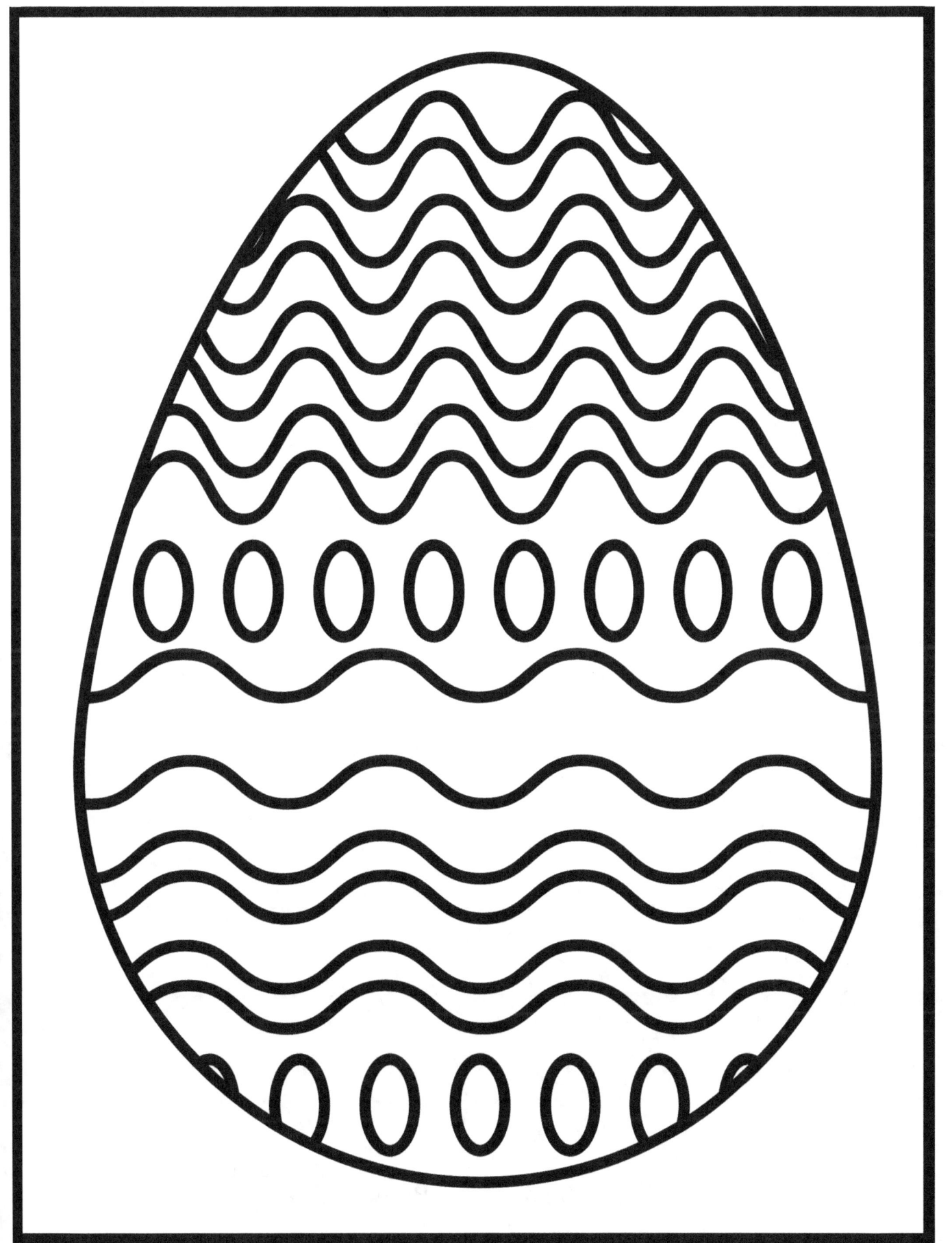

"Wavey Oval Large Patterned Egg"

HAPPY EASTER

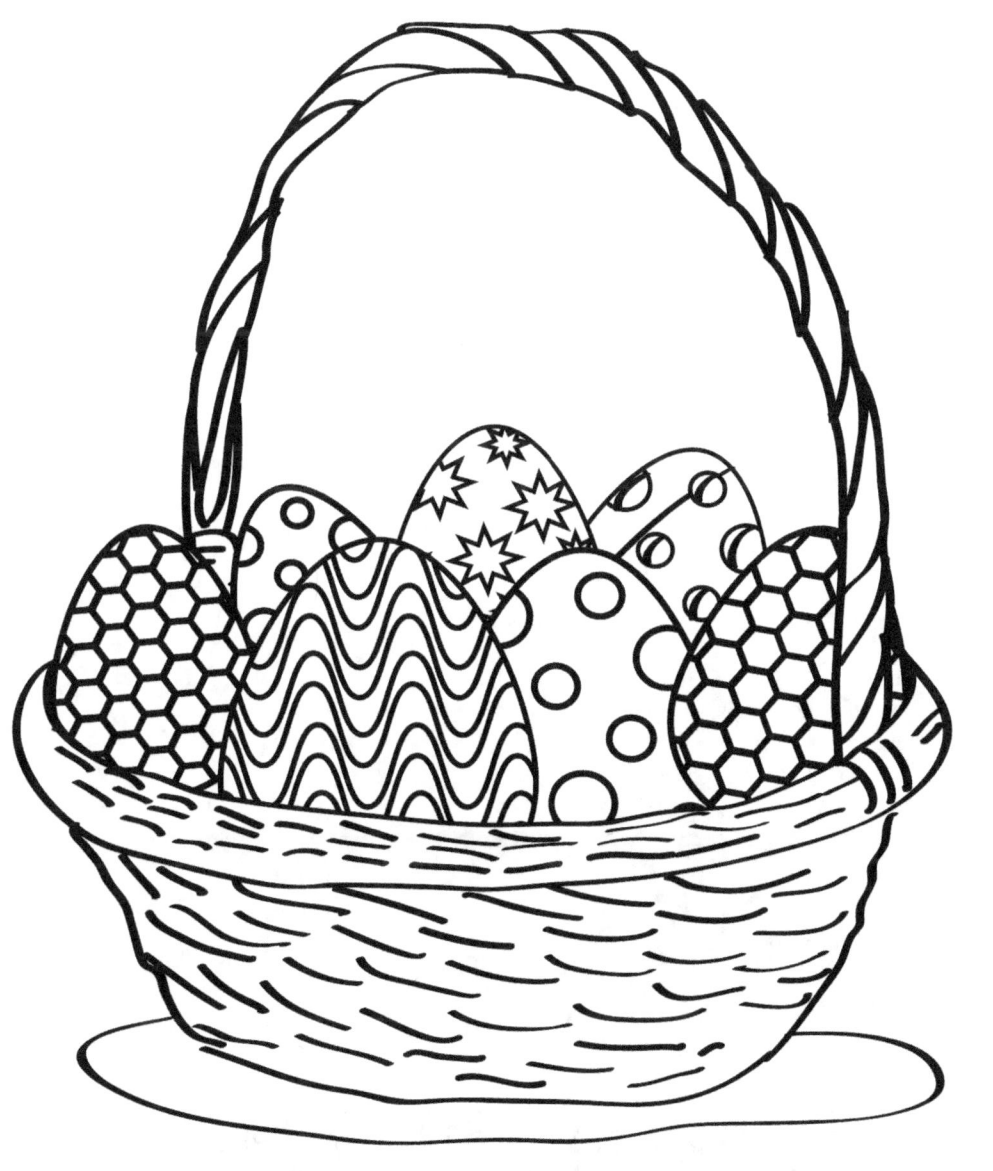

"Happy Easter: Basket Of Eggs"

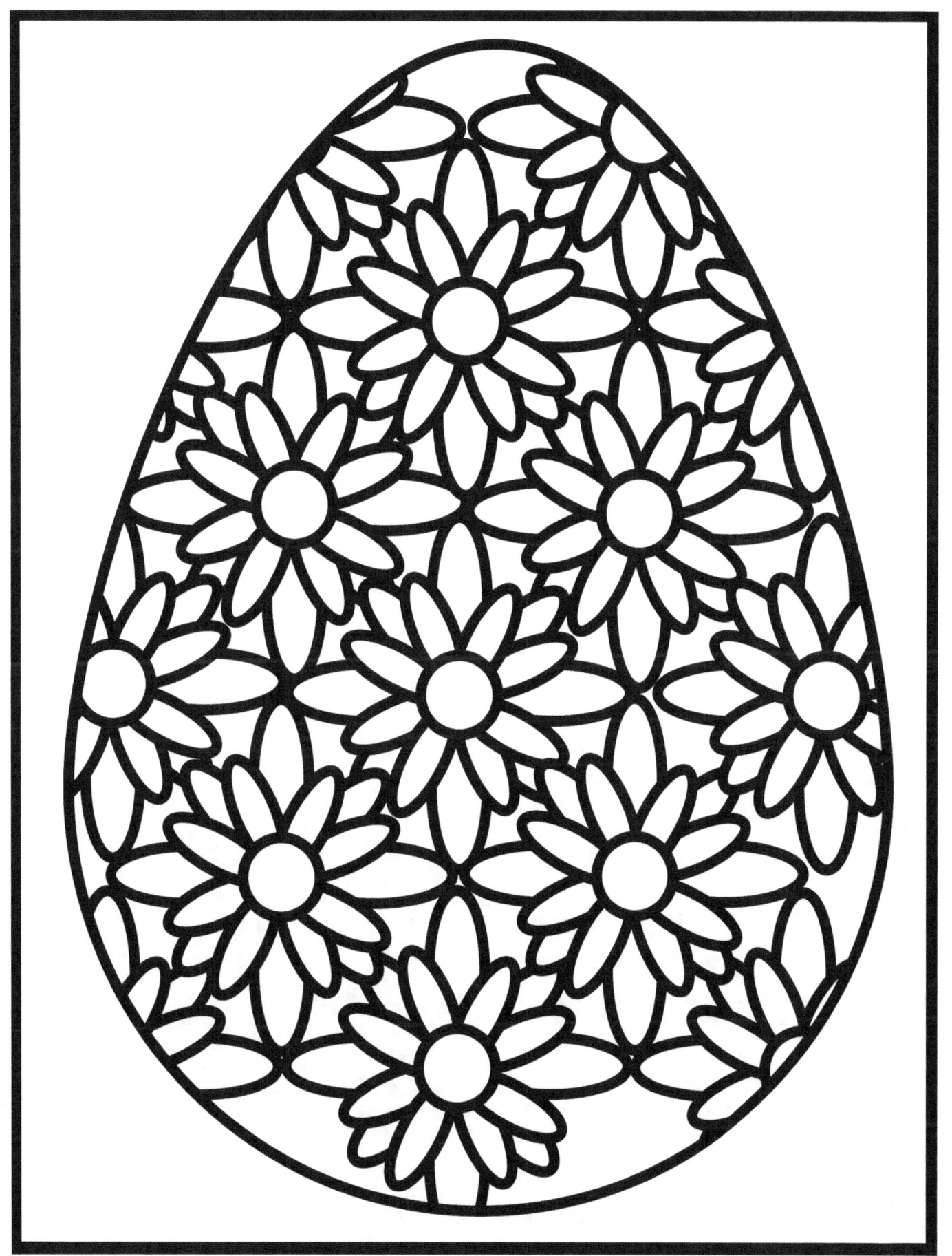

"Large Floral Patterned Egg"

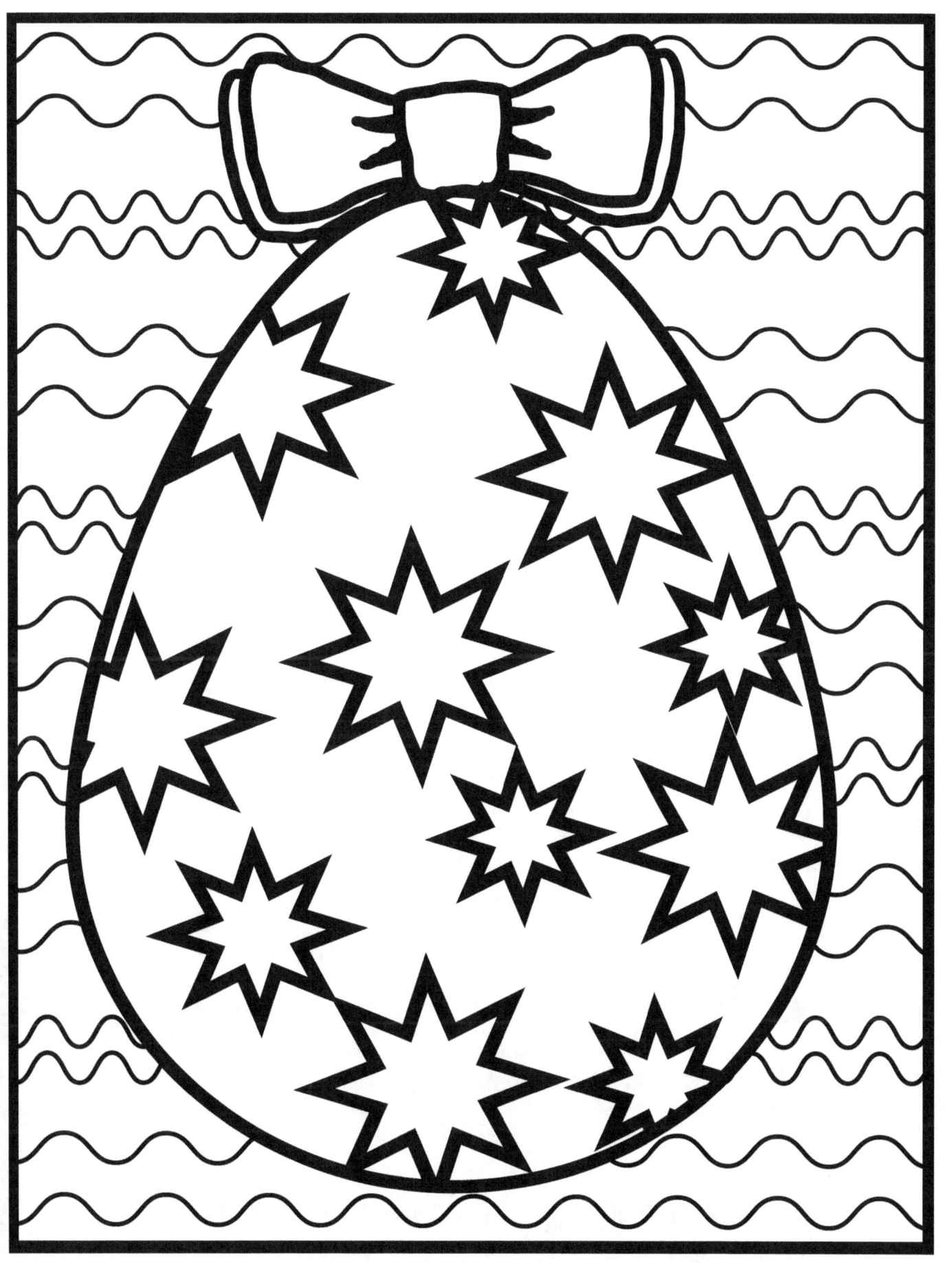

"Patterned Egg With Bow And Background"

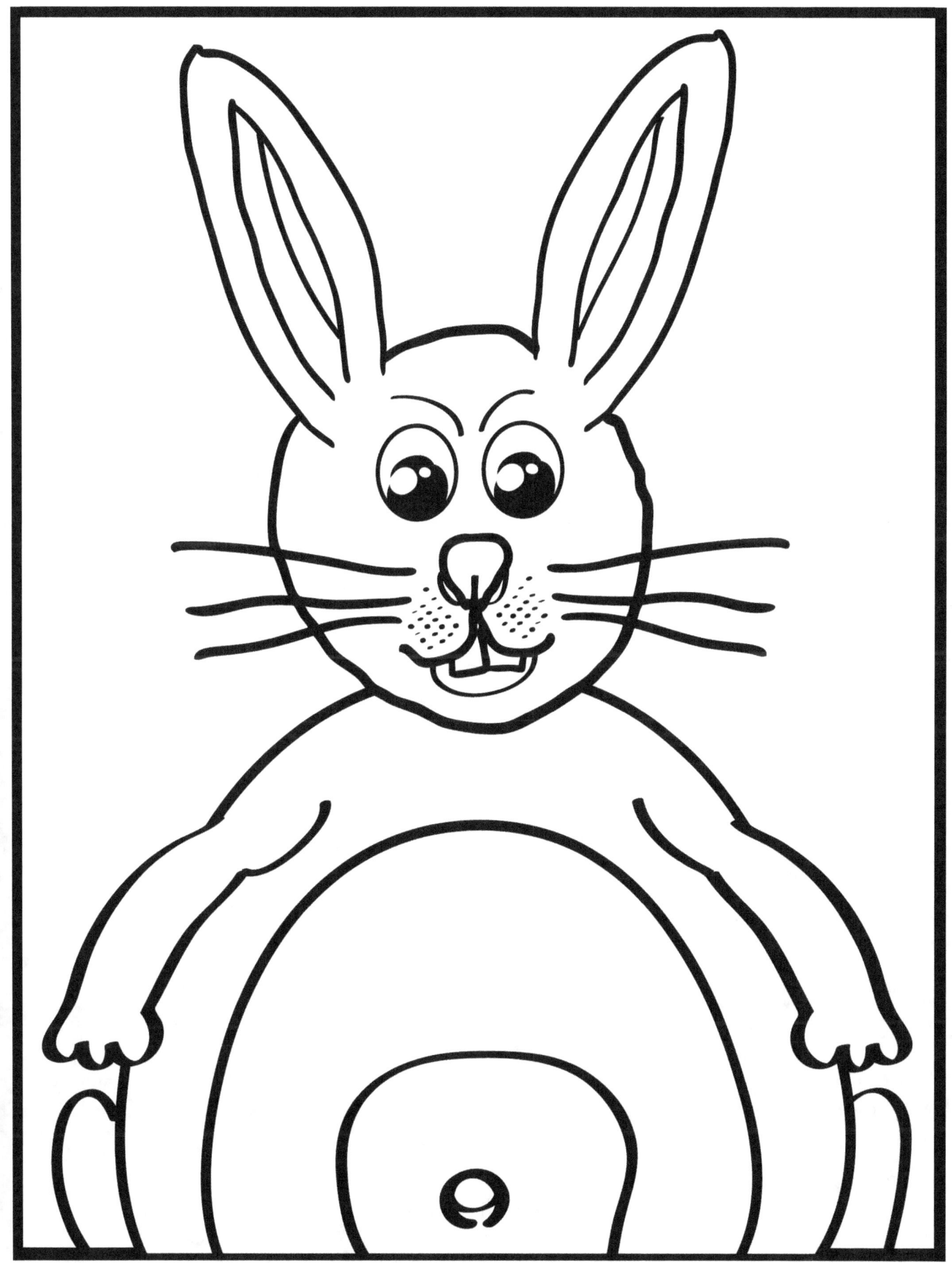

"Funny Bunny"

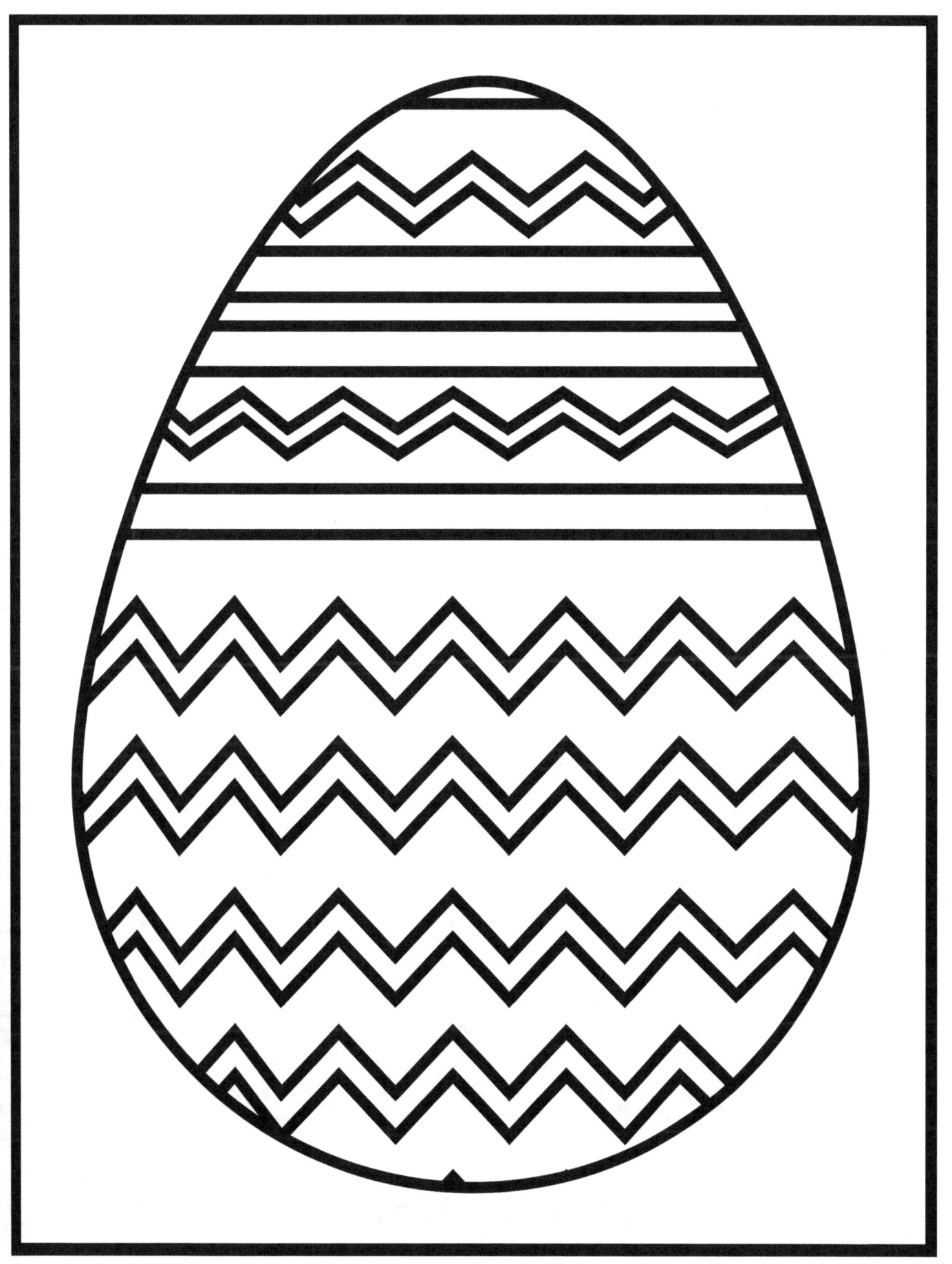

"Large Zig Zag Patterned Egg"

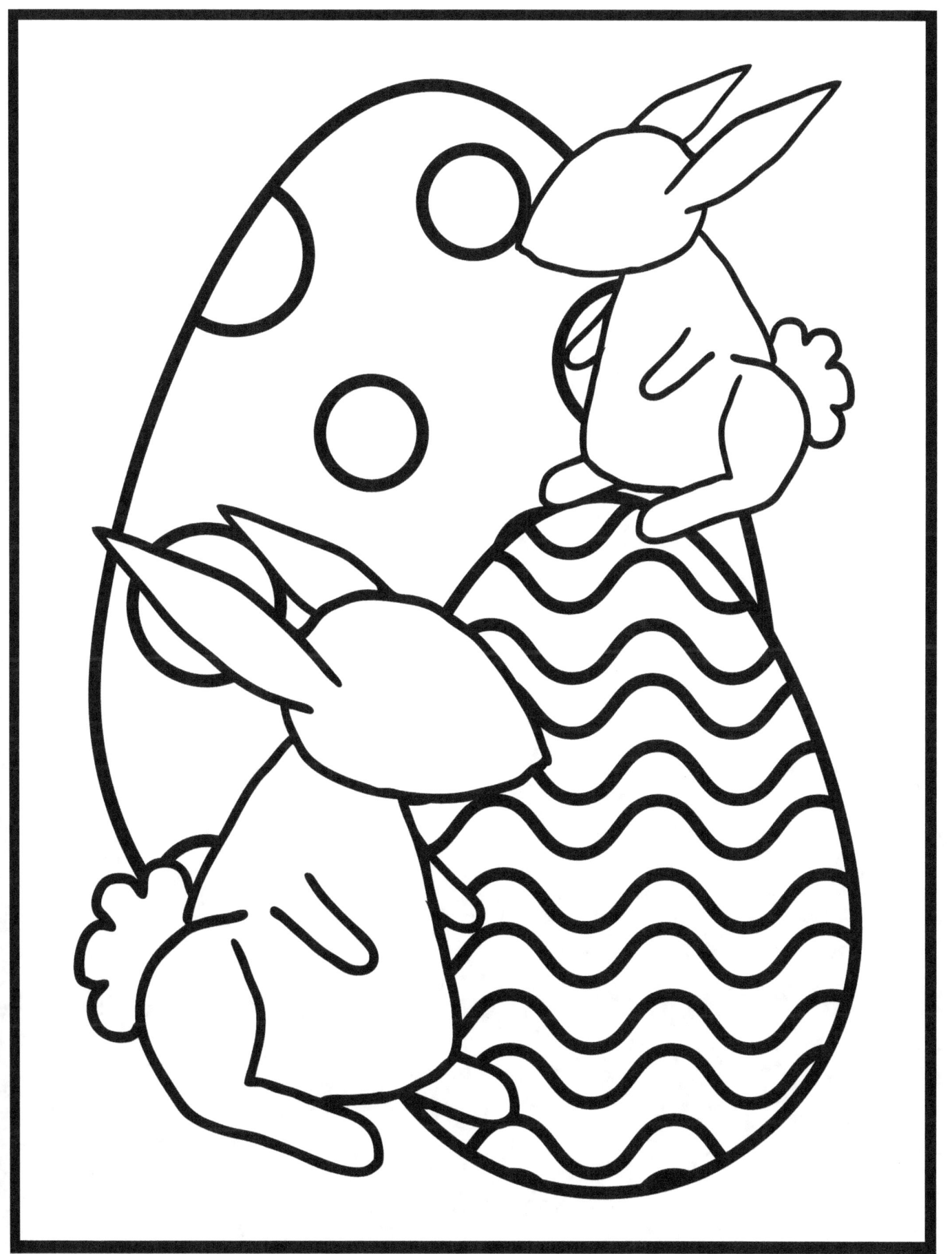

"Rabbits And Eggs"

HAPPY EASTER

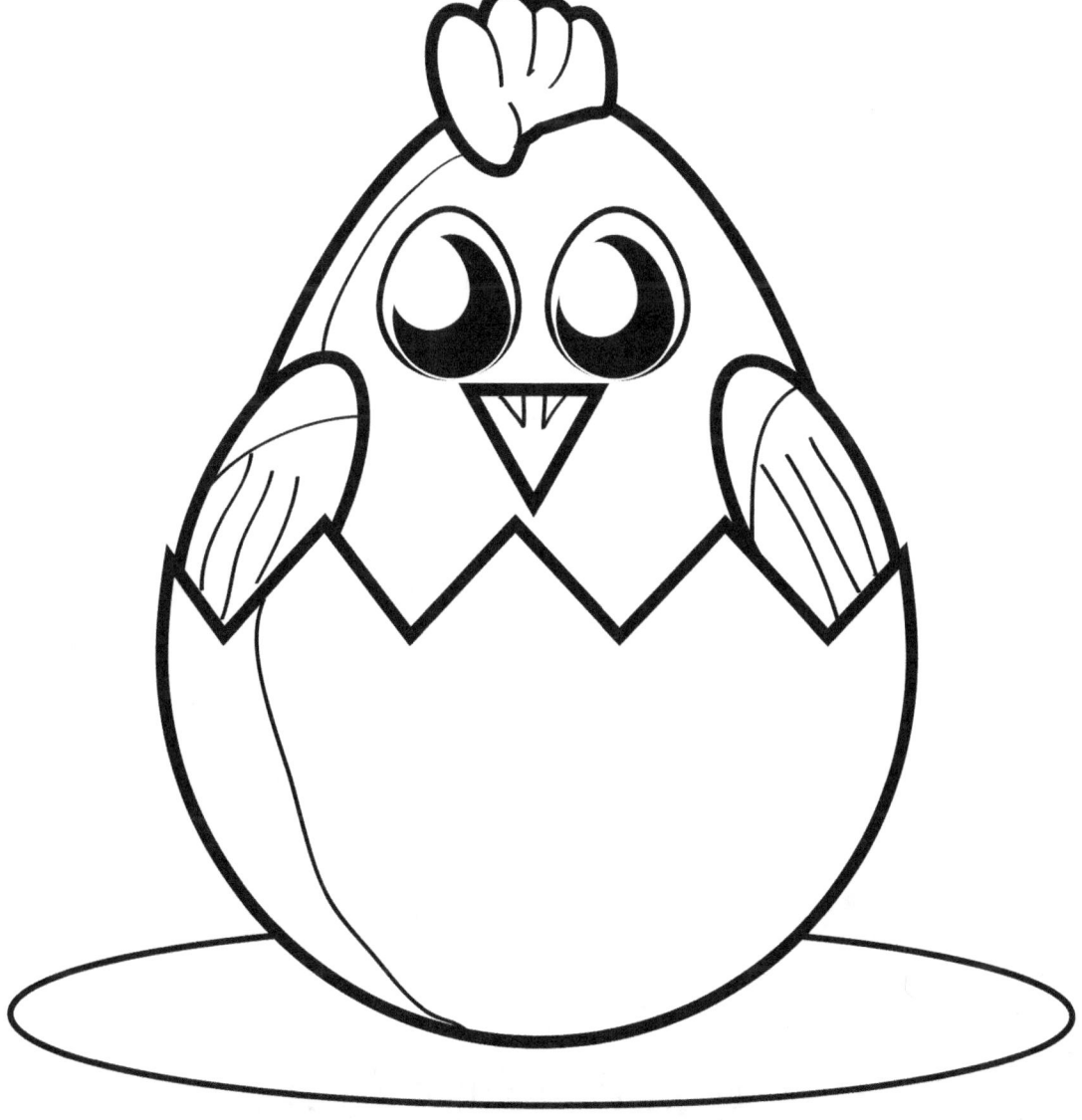

"Happy Easter: Chick In An Egg"

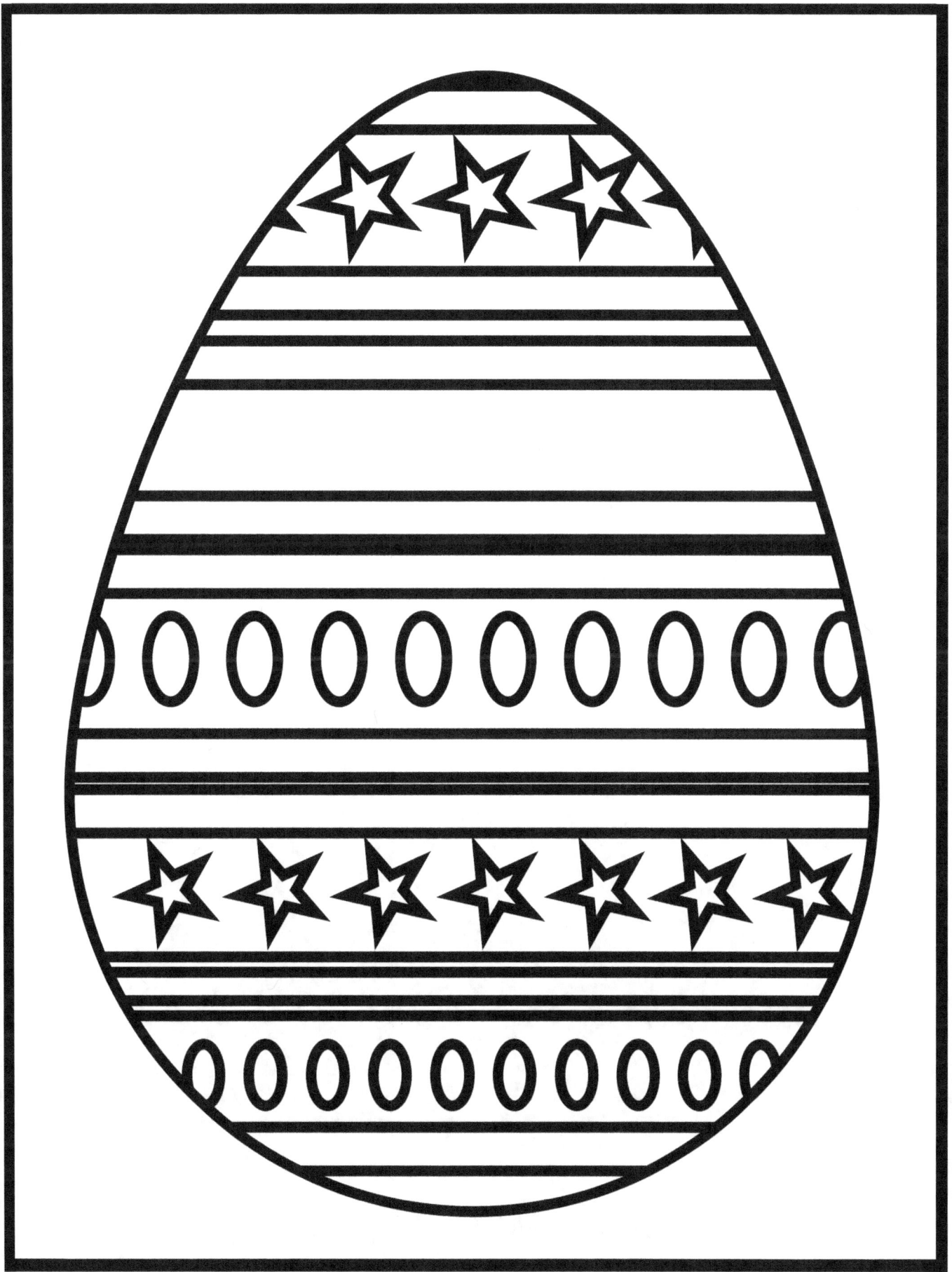

"Large Stars And Oval Patterned Egg"

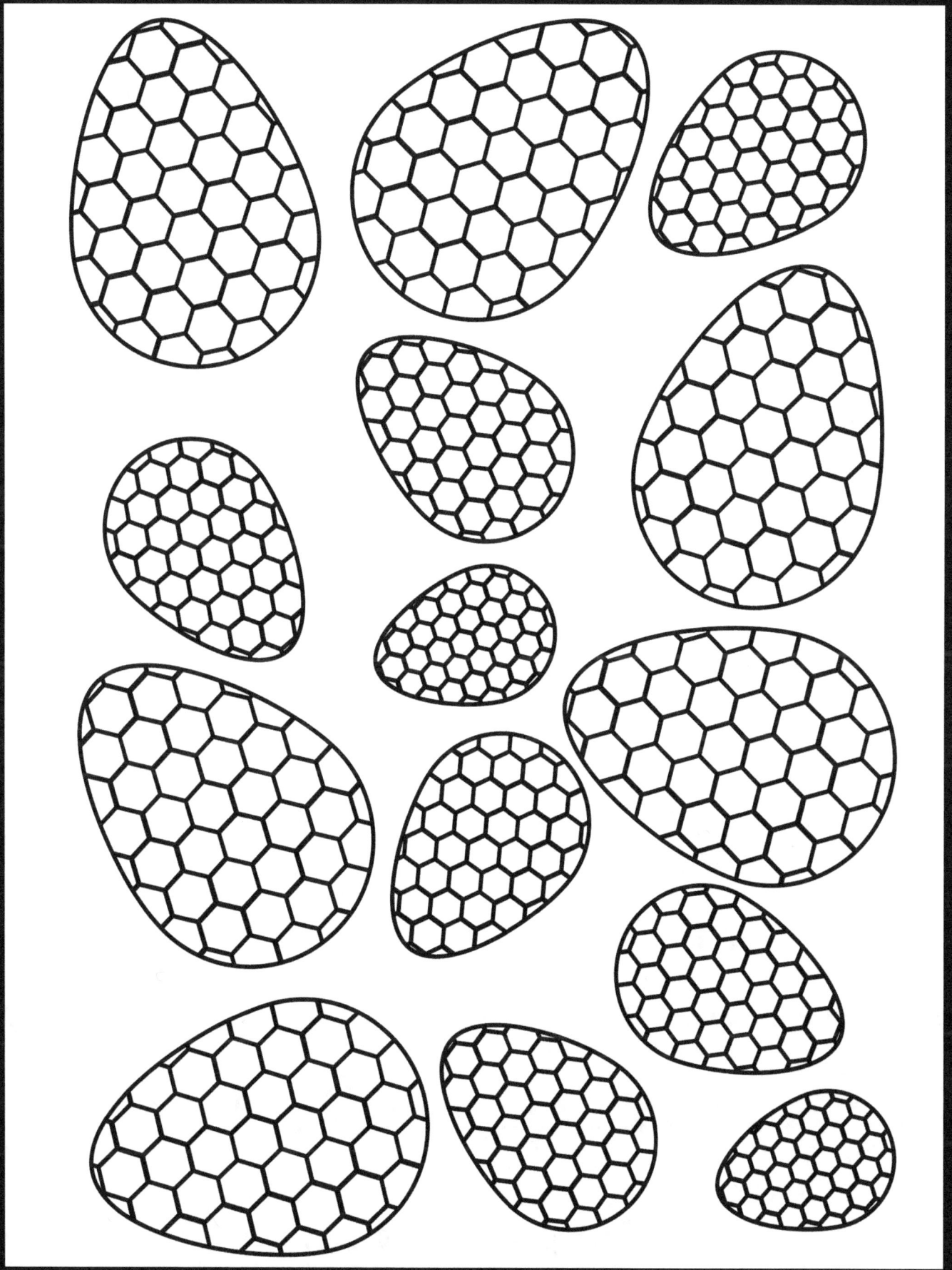

"Hexagon Patterned Eggs"

"Large Flowers And Small Bunnies"

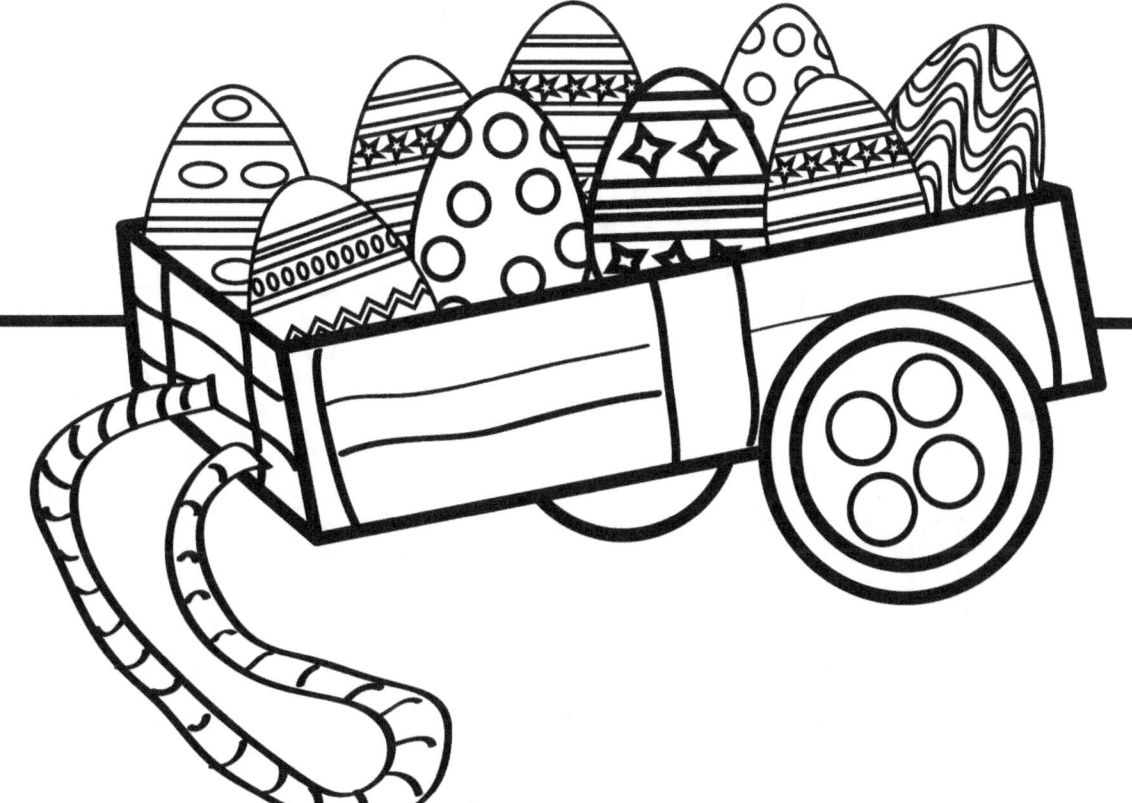

"Happy Easter: Cart With Eggs"

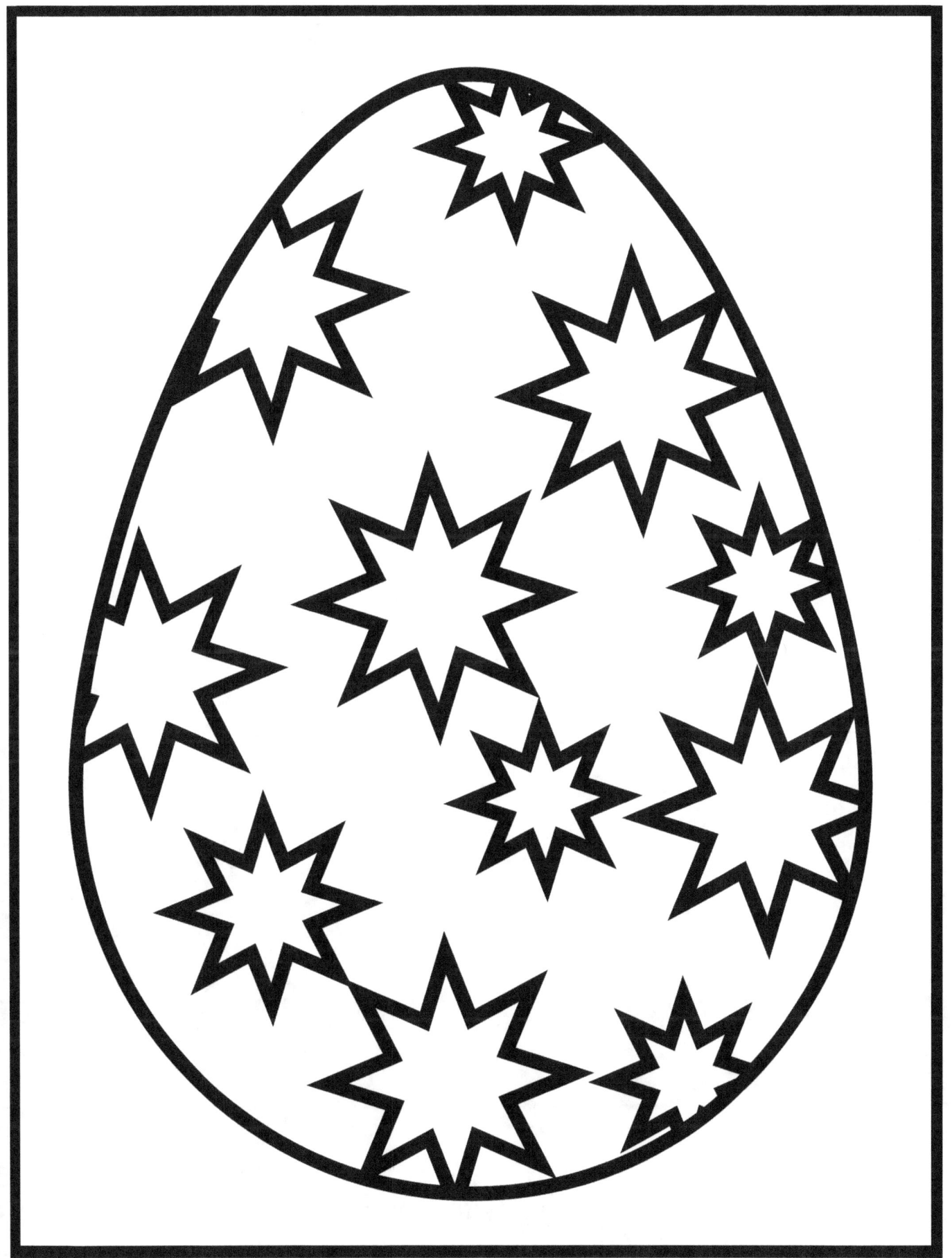

"Large Egg With Star Pattern"

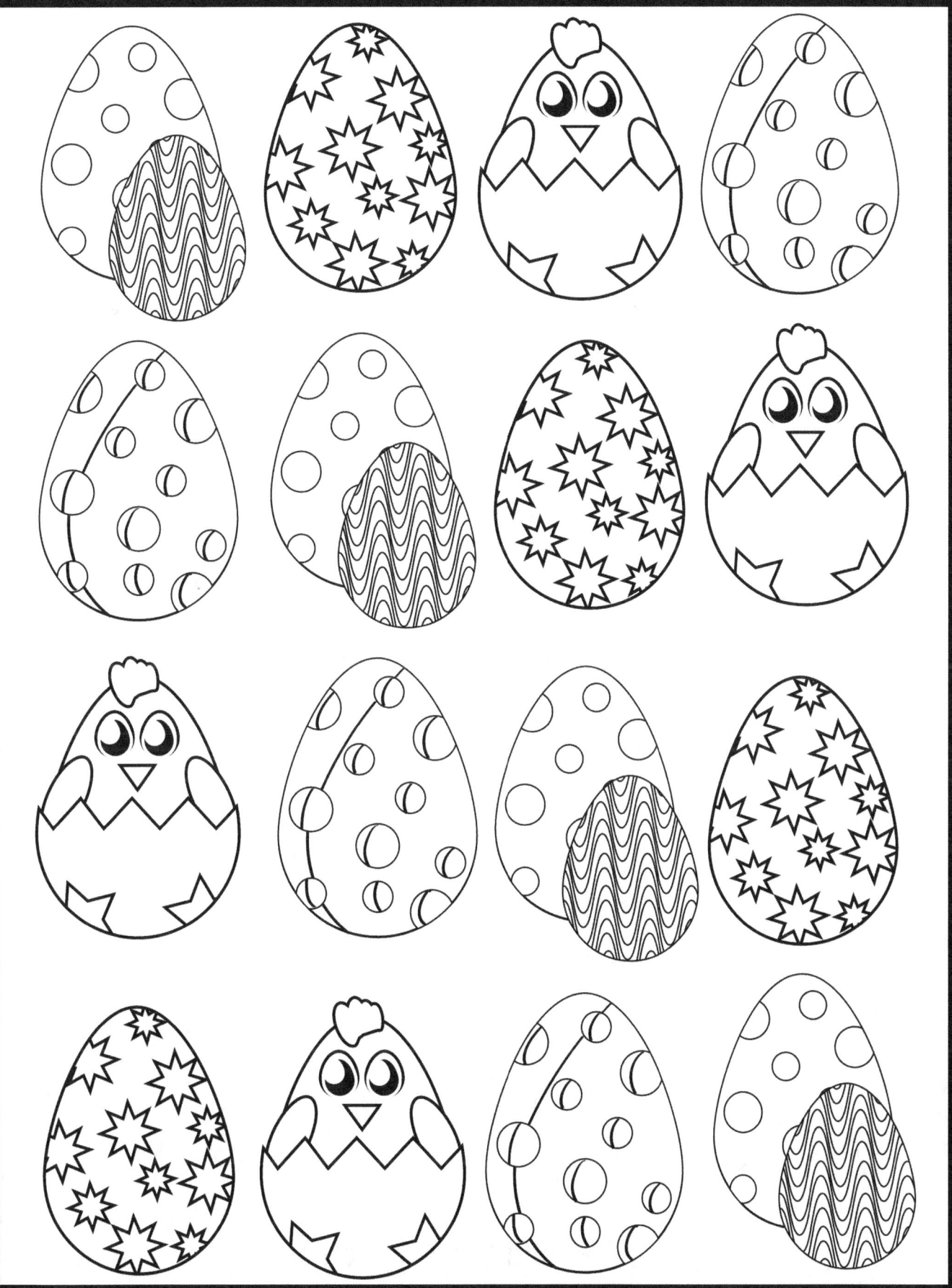

"Repeating Egg Pattern"

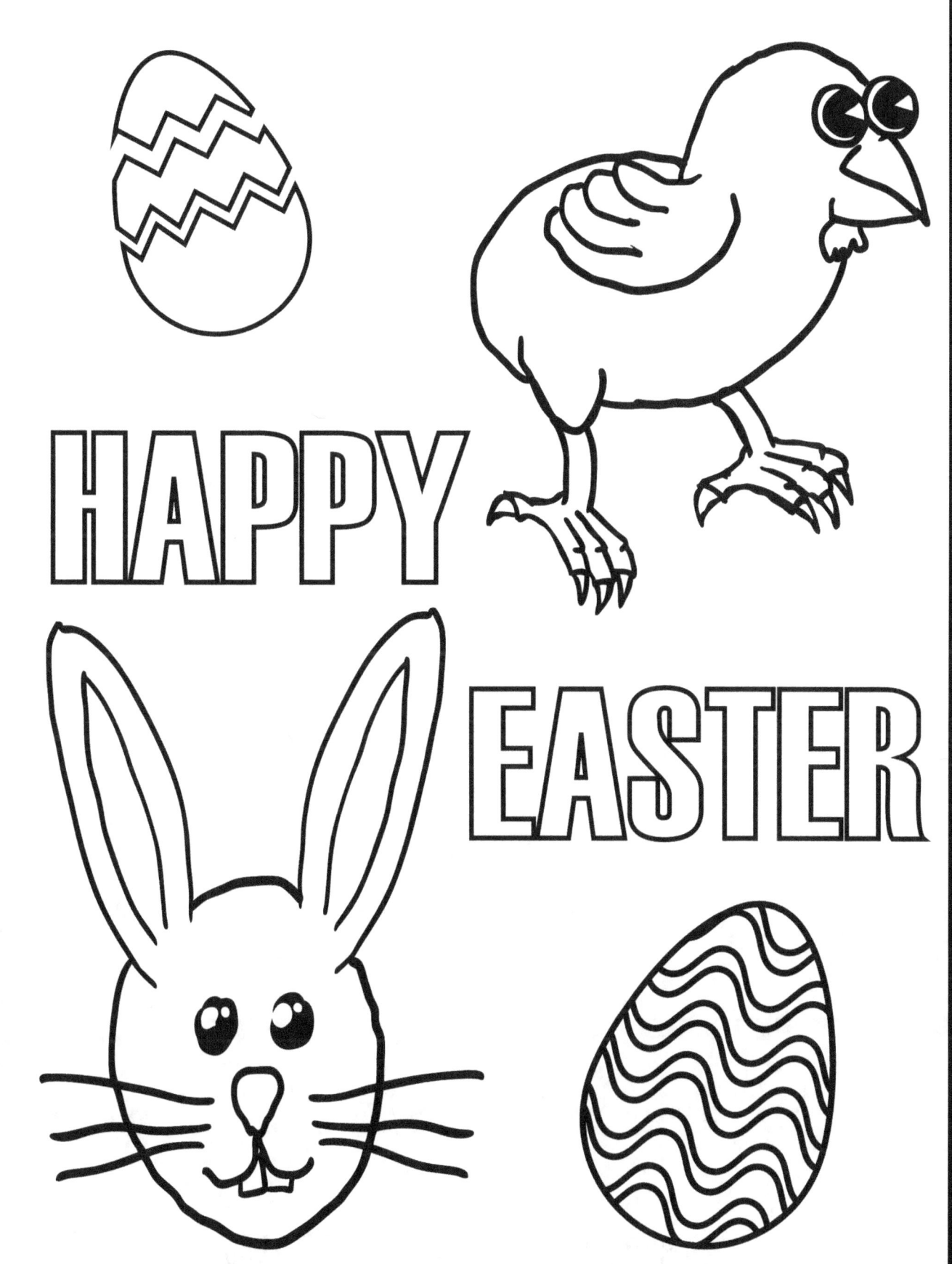

"Happy Easter: Bunny Chick And Eggs"

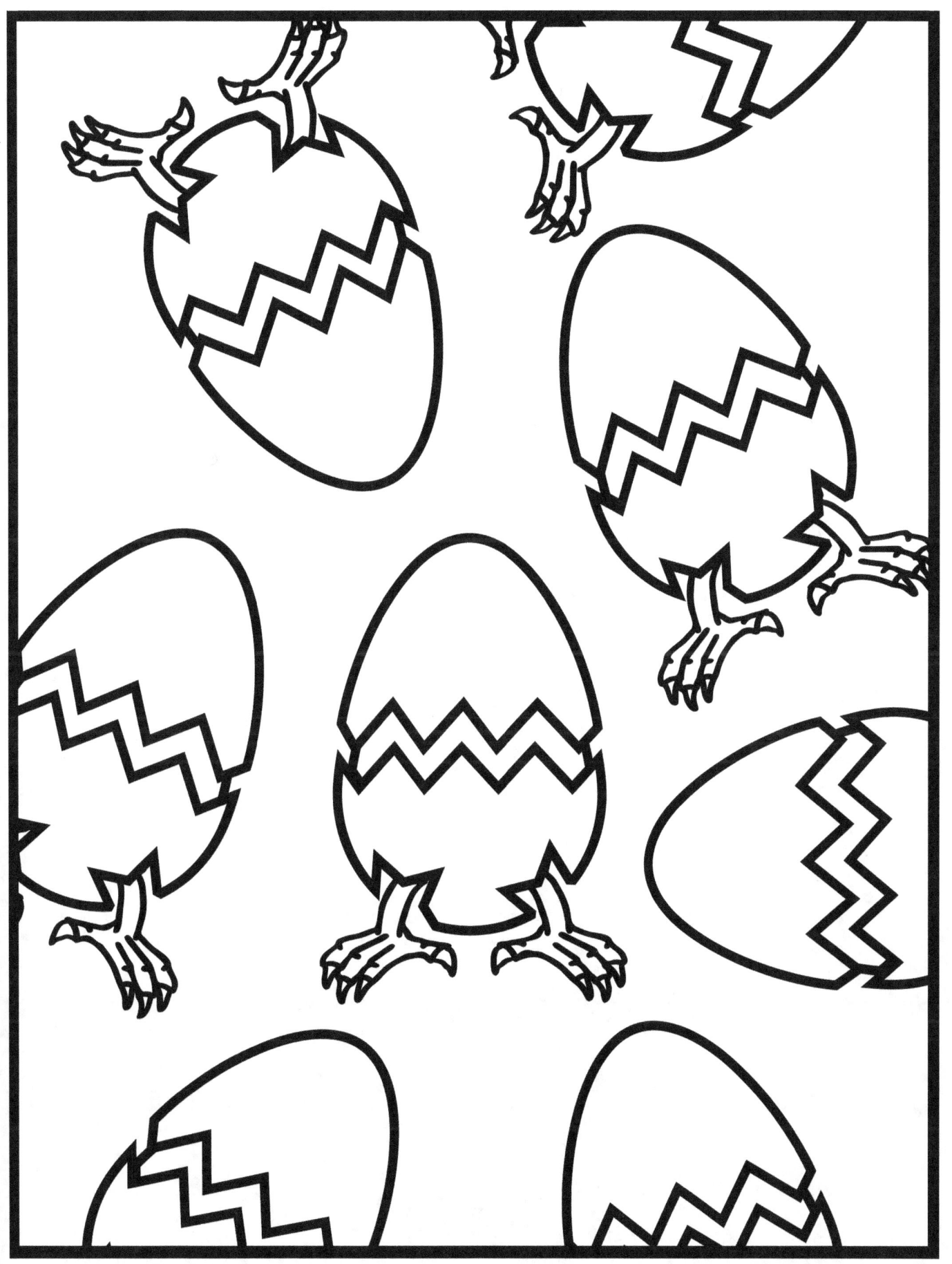

"Leggy Eggy"

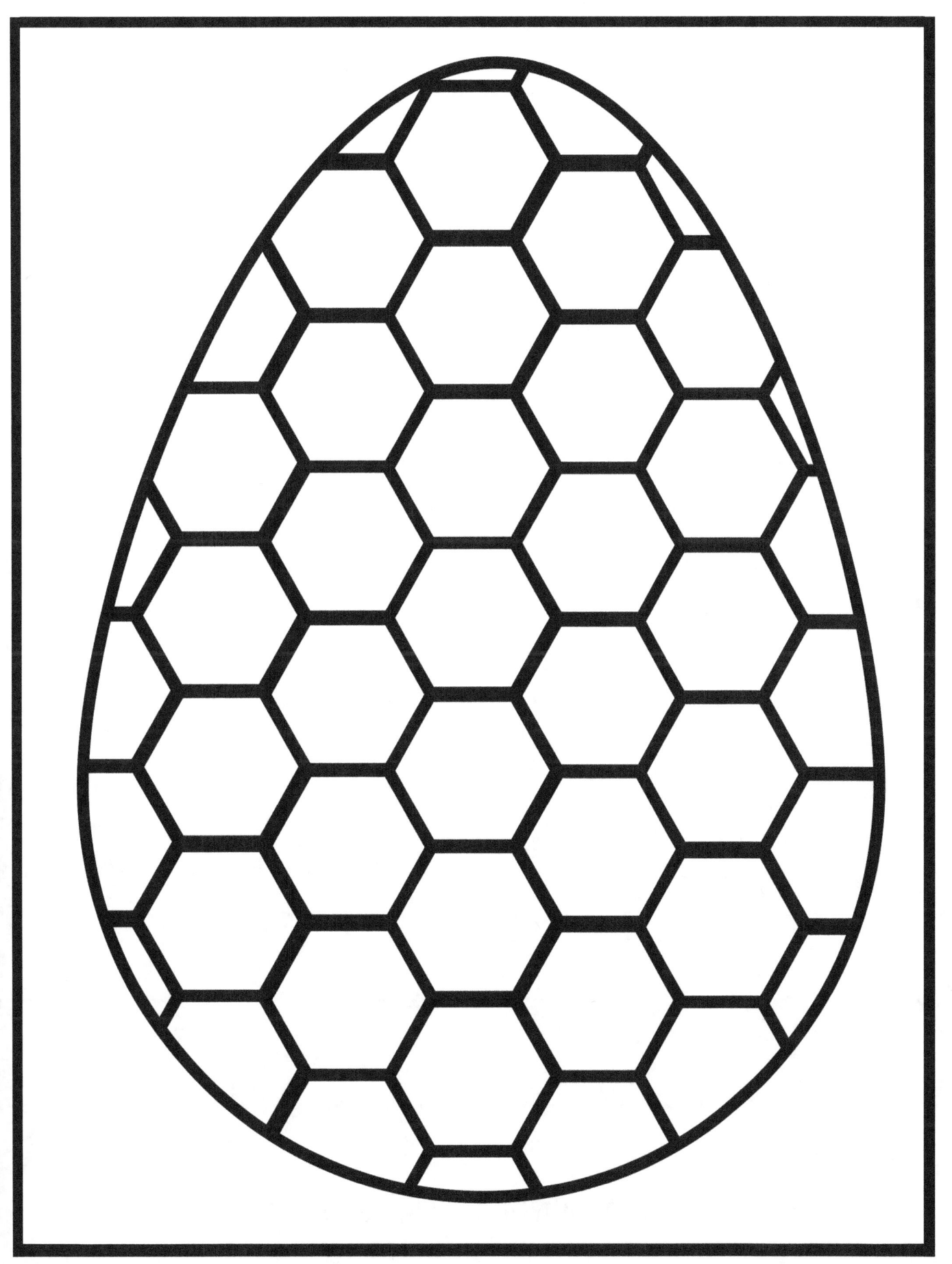

Large Patterned Egg With Scales"

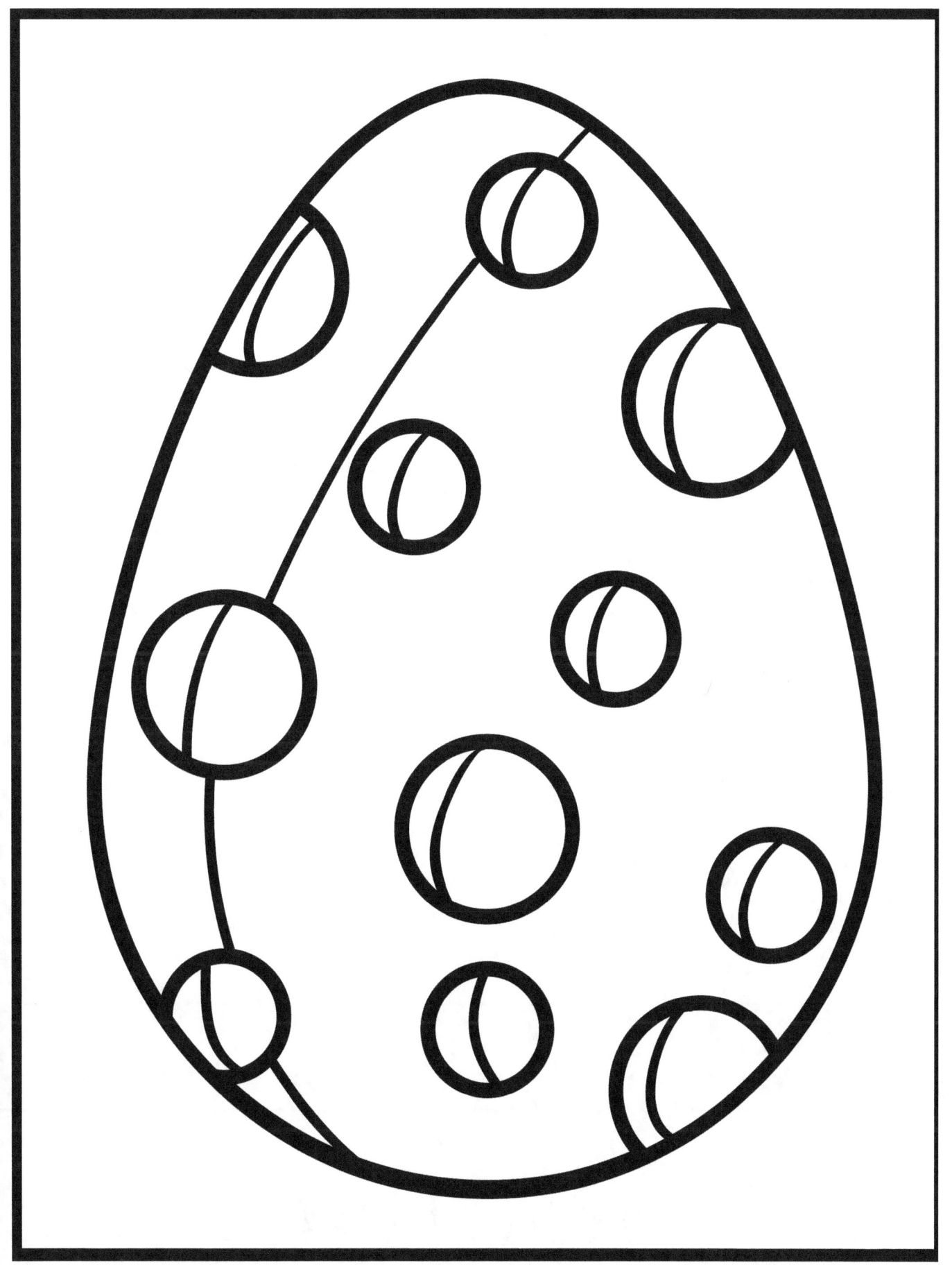

"Large Dome Patterned Egg"

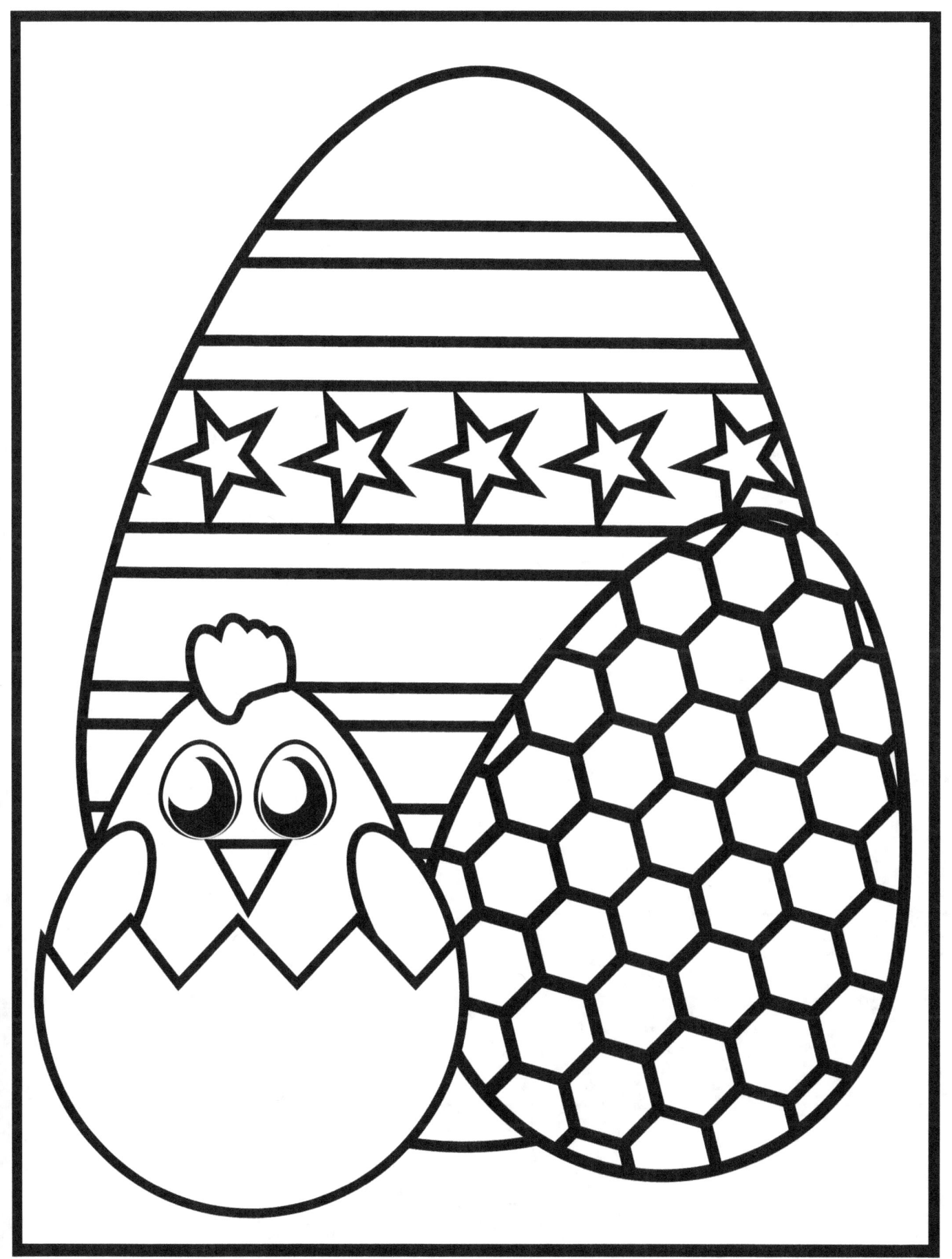

"Egg Triad"

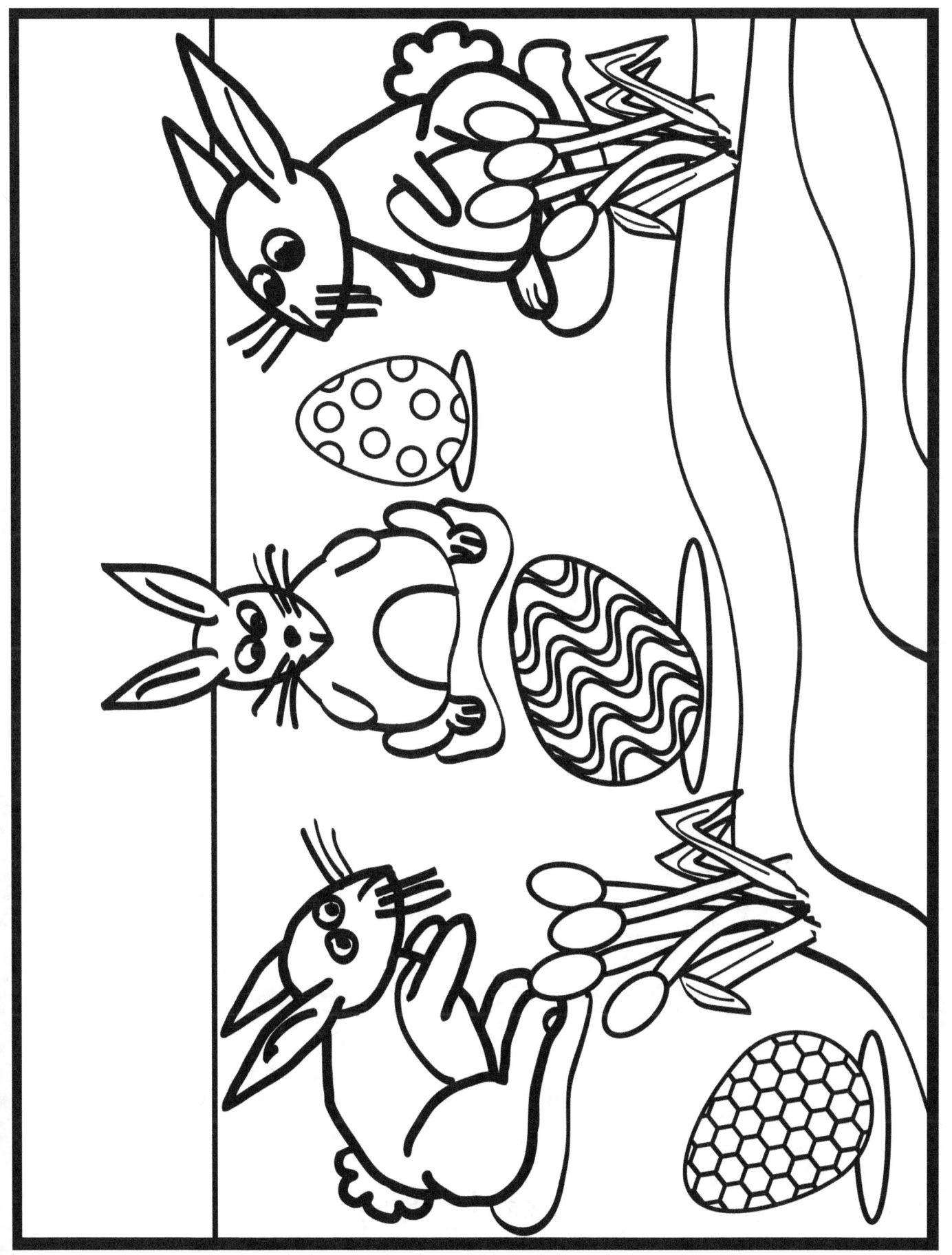

"Bunny Egg Party"